How to be a Successful PHILANDERER

A guide to down home southern wisdom

RECOMMENDED

BG Wallace

How to be a Successful

PHILANDERER

*"An instructional guide to living the
way you choose with a little down home
country wisdom thrown in."*

By

B.G. WALLACE

WORKBOOK PRESS LLC

187 E Warm Springs Rd,

Suite B285, Las Vegas, NV 89119, USA

Website: https://workbookpress.com/

Hotline: 1-888-818-4856

Email: admin@workbookpress.com

Ordering Information:

Quantity sales. Special discounts are available on quantity purchases by corporations, associations, and others. For details, contact the publisher at the address above.

Library of Congress Control Number:

ISBN-13:   978-1-963718-38-6   (Paperback Version)

                           978-1-963718-39-3   (Digital Version)

REV. DATE: 08/08/2023

To CCM and CCL, thank you for all the years you have stood by me with your support. I love you both for teaching me as much about life currently as I have taught you about days gone by.

I also dedicate his book and the wisdom it contains to my dear departed grandmother, Mellie Wallace.

"Grandma, I'll forever hold you in my heart and never forget the things you taught me."

With all my love and profound respect,
Baby Girl

Table of Contents

The Introduction 1

Where the wisdom comes from 3

Old chestnuts / Country wisdom 6

Philandering definitions 14

The five ultimate rules of philandering 16

Part 1:   21
Choosing the right person to cheat with . . . .

Part 2: 59
The matchmaking game

Part 3: 61
Telephone an email the deadly duo

Part 4: 67
Lies, who did tell, when to tell, what to tell

Part 5: 69
Time management

Part 6: 71
Philandering indicators

Part 7: 79
Things you should never do

Part 8: 85
Matters of the heart

Part 9: 91
Quit bitching and whining

Part 10: 99
A word to Mister and Mistresses

Part 11: 101
The conclusion

Introduction

Before you begin reading the pages of this guide, let us agree on two things: 1. Cheating did not begin with this book. 2. Cheating will not end with this book.

This is a guide to help you become a successful philanderer not a mandate that you start philandering. If you have purchased this book, you have already decided to philander, do not blame this book. This guide is exactly what it seems to be, a resolution to an age-old problem from a very common-sense approach employed with a little down-home country wisdom.

Since the dawn of time men and women have been philandering, in most cases unsuccessfully. This guide simply teaches you how to philander successfully if you so choose. Repeatedly I have seen people caught in secondary relationships and have their lives ruined because they were poorly equipped and uneducated philanderers. If individuals understood the proper way to philander, they would rarely, if ever, be caught. This is where I want to introduce you to the concept of "Two separate lives." If a person is going to have what I have termed a "secondary relationship," that person needs to be aware that a common mistake among philanderers is that they allow their two separate lives to meld together and create problems in both worlds. The biggest reason that people are caught cheating is that they complicate things. When you are cheating, always use the KISS rule. "Keep it secret stupid."

My dear departed grandmother, who I referred to earlier in this guide, always used to say, "never let your left hand know what your right hand is doing." I want you to take note of this chestnut because it is one of the basic rules that you should live by if you want to be a successful philanderer.

As you read this book, I invite you to make notes on your own life and your plans to be a successful philanderer. This guide is not just for those who are philanderers but also for those who may want to use this guide as a method to help them determine if you are suspicions are correct about your spouse being a philanderer. I would like for you to take a good long look at yourself and your life and make sure that being a successful philanderer is what you really want to do.

Where the Wisdom Comes From

A force to be reckoned with and a passion and heart to match, that was my grandma Mellie. She was a very plainspoken woman with a heart of pure gold. She loved the way she lived, hard. Mellie had a zest for life that kept her going through the good times and the bad. She was not a student of human nature she was the professor. If there was anything that a person needed to know about life, love, relationships, men and or women the person to go to and the person that everyone came to for advice was Mellie

Mellie was married to the same man for over 50 years and there was never a time in my life that I would not see the unconditional love for her in his eyes. There was a time in his life when he was seeing another woman But because of who my grandmother was and how she chose to live life it brought him home to her with a solemn promise that he would never stray again. Mind you, it did not hurt at all that she caught him in a compromising position and took a Coleman whip to him. This just goes to show you that no matter how much a person loves you they can only be pushed so far.

Now, I know that currently not just men but women who are also doing their philandering. One thing that I have learned over the years is that people are going to do just what they are going to do and no matter how much you try to keep them on lockdown they will find a way to cheat. Looking back on all the things that my grandmother tried to teach me when I was growing up one thing has remained a constant in her assessment of the human condition: "No matter how much things change they always stay the same when it comes to relationships."

This manuscript was not just written for Philanderers, but it was also written for those who want to see the reality of their lives and to see clearly what is ahead of them and why. My grandmother would have wanted it that way. I think that it would make her smile to know that her wisdom continues to make a difference in the lives of others. In her day there was not a woman or man in town that did not come to her at one time or another to seek her sage advice about their relationships. I can remember as a little girl being in church and someone would pull grandma away for a private chat about their relationship issues, and no matter what that issue was grandma always had a way to fix it for them to bring a little more peace to their lives.

My hope is that everyone who reads this book takes something good away from it. If you are unhappy with your life, then change it. If you think that you want to engage in a secondary relationship, then do what you do Booboo, but do it the right way. Never let what you want destroy what you have. No matter which way it goes you will know that you are doing what you want and what is right in your life for now. You will know that your decision comes from good information and a good plan A, after all, if you do not want to go to Plan B (lying), then you had better have a damn good plan A.

Old Chestnuts / Country Wisdom

I talked a lot about my grandmother Mellie in the previous pages now I want to give you some of her best chestnuts AKA country wisdom; Grandma always used to say:

"Baby girl, it's a good thing to meet your problems eye to eye, but it's a better thing to come out with your hide still on your backside."

"Baby girl, if you keep joking at your problems and sooner or later, they're going to bite you on the ass."

"Baby girl, a man's going to do what a man's going to do, it doesn't matter how much you run him down or try to see what he's doing he's going to be a man."

"Baby girl, if you go outside and threw a stick, you will hit ten men who would give you their dick faster than they would get you a glass of ice water."

"Baby girl, you can lie to your family and your friends, but you can't lie to yourself if you were doing something you don't want nobody to know about then you know what's wrong."

"Baby girl, if you lay down with dogs you get up with fleas."

"Baby girl, what you do in the dark always comes to the light. "

"Baby girl, ain't nothing open late at night but the Juke joint and some woman's legs."

"Baby girl, if you keep telling a woman how good your man is all the time, she just might want to try him."

"Baby girl, a man or a woman gone from home all the time is eventually going to bring something home they didn't leave with."

"Baby girl, don't chase a rabbit in the Woods when you got a chicken right there in your own hen house."

"Baby girl, don't let your mouth write a check your ass can't cash."

"Baby girl, a person never missed the water till the well runs dry."

"Baby girl, every woman knows a man who is sick of their ass."

"Baby girl, look in the bed before you get in it that way you know what you're dealing with."

"Baby girl, anything A man or woman can do with you they can do to you."

"Baby girl, don't call on the Lord to clean up a mess you made on your own."

"Baby girl don't ever let a man tell you more than once that he doesn't want you. The first time he says it should be the last time he said it to you."

"Baby girl, ain't no fun when the rabbit's got the gun."

"Baby girl, never let a man walk on you like a rug at the front door."

"Baby girl, never let your right hand know what your left hand is doing."

"Baby girl, when you give a dog a bone, don't be surprised when he starts chewing on it."

"Baby girl, questions without cause never get asked."

"Baby girl, that boy is slick as possum fat and just as greasy."

"Baby girl, nothing wants and no good woman, but a no-good man and the other side is the same."

"Baby girl, ain't a soul on earth who ain't stepped out

once that ain't willing to step out twice and if they step out twice it's because they like the feeling the first time."

"Baby girl, Ain't nothing worse than a man that thinks too highly of himself because that means he thinks nothing of you. "

"Baby girl, never let what is between his legs rule what is in your head, because you are bound to mess them both up."

"Baby girl, old dogs like fresh meat too."

"Baby girl, your head will hold on to anything your heart tells it to."

"Baby girl if you don't want a stray dog at your door don't feed it."

"Baby girl never ask a man where he's going or where he's been because he just might tell you."

"Baby girl, I know he thinks she slick but he could use another greasing."

"Baby girl you need to watch were you step because you might end up stepping in shit."

Baby Girl's Chestnut

In the great tradition of my dearly departed grandma, I would like to impart my own chestnuts that are appropriate for today's relationship climate.

"When you're leaving a relationship pack your feels before you pack your belongings."

"There is nothing wrong in letting a man ware the pants in a relationship but remind him who irons those pants."

"A relationship is only as good as the foundation it is built on."

"Advising a person over and over that you will leave them is like pointing a load gun at them over and over... They do not believe you until you pull the trigger."

Bull shit is still bull shit no matter how many roses you can grow with it."

"Never pick up something that you can't carry."

"Men are like city buses; one comes by every 15 minutes. It is up to you if you want to take a ride."

Great Philanderers in History

When I say that cheating did not begin with this manuscript, and it will not end with this manuscript I come with receipts.

Let us begin with Casanova; and yes, Casanova was a real person. Giacomo Girolamo Casanova was born in Venice in 1725. In my opinion he was the original Beelzebub's Brother Lady's Man. This brother was a schemer and a charmer. One of the main driving forces in his life appeared to be sex. He was 11 years old when he engaged in his first sexual foray and continued to practice with many of the female population of Venice until he was no longer able to get it up. It is said that he was a great fan of cunnilingus.

King Charles II: It is written that King Charles was such a Ho that he almost bankrupted the entire kingdom and when he suspected that he may be beheaded for his mismanagement of the country, he fled to France where he proceeded to screw his way thru most of the female population of France.

George Gordon Byron aka "Lord Byron": Lord Byron who was overweight, had a club foot and was considered basic looking, managed to seduce countless men and women, young and old, married, and single. Double Ho!... Just goes to show that there is someone for everyone.

Pablo Picasso: A talented artist and an even greater philanderer.   Picasso died in 1973 at the age of 92. Between life and death, he managed to dally with as many as 2,500 lovers.   Now that is philandering par excellence. He was into women like Satan's Sisters Desperate and Gullible.   Picasso left his first wife for his pregnant mistress, who was 30 years his junior.   He refused to acquiesce to his mistress's demand that he divorce his first wife (Beelzebub Brother Pimp behavior), then he left her and married again at 79, at which time he proceeded to pursue other women in full view of wife number two.   When he died, he had a statue of his first wife installed on his grave causing his mistress to hang herself four years after his death. Now that was a memorable male member.

Those are just a few of the more notorious philanderers in history but I would be remiss if I did not make honorable mention to the following philanderers.

John F. Kennedy AKA "JFK":   A US President who allegedly dallied or diddled his mistress(s) in the White House.

John Wilkes, not to be confused with John Wilkes Booth, was an English radical journalist, politician, magistrate, essayist and soldier and a true believer in free love two hundred years before its popularity.   It is alleged that he was a legendary lothario. He was said to be the ugliest man in all of England". Wilkes embraced the judgement and said that his looks was the reason that he became so adept at seducing women with his character rather than his looks. He maintained his charms could beat any other man's looks when a came to getting a woman. It is said that he was often correct in his assessment.

Peter Alekseyevich Romanov AKA "Peter the Great": He was a true Beelzebub Brother Player and slept around frequently.   It is alleged that when his second wife decided to take a lover of her own, Peter became so enraged, he had the lover's head separated from his body and the head placed in a jar. He then had the head presented to his wife as a reminder to her to remain faithful.

Philandering Definitions

In this manual I will refer often to some definitions that you will want to bear in mind:

1. **Philanderer:** a person that has a secondary relationship in secret.
2. **Successful philanderer:** a person who has an ongoing secondary relationship and has not been caught.
3. **Stupid philanderer:** a person that has a secondary relationship and is caught quite often.
4. **Defendant philanderer:** a person who is a party to his or her divorce proceedings because they were a stupid philanderer.
5. **Broke philanderer:** a person who has secondary relationships outside of marriage, has been caught and taken to the cleaners by his or her spouse in the divorce.
6. **Mistress:** a woman who engages in an affair with a married man or woman.
7. **Mister:** a man who engages in an affair with a married man or woman.
8. **Secondary relationship:** a relationship conducted outside of a person's primary relationship and is carried on in secret.
9. **Separate lives:** multiple lives that are carried on

independently of each other.

10. **Primary relationship:** Marriage or a committed non marriage relationship.

11. **Chestnut:** an all saying as told by my grandmother.

The Five Ultimate Rules
of Philandering

One of the first things that my grandmother said to me when I told her that I suspected that my husband was cheating and the reasons why was "baby girl, I know he thinks he's being slick, but he could use another greasing." What you will read are all the things that men and women do not do when they are cheating and the things that their partners notice to make them suspect infidelity. You can have all the plans in the world, all the angles covered, and still get caught cheating. But that event is less likely when you have a great plan. "Plan the work and work the plan."

Rule #1: : keep your mouth shut: no one needs to know about your secondary relationship because if they know they will have one of six reactions:

Jealousy: in which case, they cannot wait to tell any that will listen All that they know about you.

Envy: in which case they are also jealous, and they cannot wait to tell any that will listen, all they know about you.

Righteous indignation: in which case they cannot wait to preach to you about the bad turn your life has taken.

Maliciousness: in which case they have never liked you, they are envious and jealous of you and therefore they cannot wait to tell all that they know or think they know about you. In many cases they scurry over to tell the spouse first.

Just a big mouth: in which case they will tell all they know about you just because they know something new, and they can.

Stupid: in which case they assume that because you told them your secret it is OK for them to tell others.

Rule #2: never leave a paper trail:

More primary relationships have been ended and divorces have begun because of written evidence of infidelity than I can tell you about. As my grandma used to say, 'remember something baby girl, questions without cause never get asked." For the learning impaired that simply means if a spouse or significant other does not have a reason to ask a question they never will. A paper trail is one of the things that always causes questions to be asked. Little pieces of paper with numbers and no names are a dead giveaway. It is like saying "hey spouse, look I'm cheating come and catch me."

Rule #3: never call your mister or mistress from your home telephone:

Stay off your home telephone with your mister or mistress. I have heard more stories than I care to tell where men and women were caught cheating because of the telephone. When you involve this little mechanical wonder that is in your home, you are just begging to be caught. You are doing the thing that I have already warned you about…. merging your two lives and that is never a good thing. Again, this is the perfect time to wrap your brain around the concept of two separate lives. This rule includes your mobile phone as well. If you think that your spouse is not checking your cellular device, please think again. I can assure you that your spouse can tell you the last 10 calls that you made from your personal communication device. Cheating can sometimes be a rich man's or rich woman's game. Invest in a cell phone that your spouse does not know about.

Rule #4: never give your mister or mistress access to your primary life. Too much information provided to a mistress or mister always comes back to bite one in the ass. Like my dear old grandma used to say, "if you give a dog a bone, don't be surprised when they chew on it."

Rule #5: Know who you are sleeping with before you sleep with them. Like my dear old grandma used to say, "baby girl, when it comes to loving look in the bed before you get in it, that way you'll know what you're dealing with." Now again for the learning impaired, that simply means you cannot sleep with just anyone because you do not know what type of person you are dealing with.

To that end, I would like you to look at just who you have been sleeping with. I have given a name to these misters and mistresses; they are Satan's Sisters and Beelzebub's Brothers.

PART 1:
Choosing the Right Person to Philander With

Ever since I was a young girl, I was, other than Grandma, that person that people told their "dark doings" to. I believe in their eyes I was a substitute for my grandmother, and I possessed her wisdom. I can remember being barely in my teens and Mrs. Jenkins telling me all about her affair with old man Davis or Mr. Tisdale telling me about his affair with Mrs. Libby. All these stories gave me a wealth of knowledge about why people cheat, how they cheat and most importantly how to be successful at it.

Mellie was incredibly wise and a very straightforward woman and if she said something, you could bet dollars to donuts that it was true. One of the first things that she ever taught me about relationships was about cheating. She would say, "Baby girl, ain't a soul on earth who ain't stepped out once that ain't willing to step out twice and if they step out twice it's because they like the feeling the first time." Translation: People who philander cheap because they like it and not for any other reason. The reasons that you get from them are only their justification.

Choosing the correct person to philander with is a matter of just one thing knowing the type of person you are sleeping with before you sleep with them. The first thing that attracts you to any other person is looks. But jumping into bed with someone based solely on looks is always trouble. You could be jumping into bed with an attractive psycho. This is a good time to refer to my grandmother's earlier quote: "look in the bed before you get in it that way, you'll know what you're dealing with." The best way to avoid the mental and physical problems that can Occur is to find out a bit about that person before you hop into bed with them. Be patient! Do this right and the sex will "come."

Be a gentleman or a lady. The fact that you are, will get you points towards your goal and the fact that you are asking questions of that person is a good thing to them because they will look at this as you being interested in who they are and not just trying to get them into bed. Do not be obvious like a farmer looking into the mouth of a horse he is planning to buy. Have a conversation with that perspective partner. Philandering is not mutually exclusive to a person being a "dog or whore." Philandering means that your taste buds for variety in life are well developed. This brings us to the type of mister or mistress that is suitable for your needs.

The first thing that you need to know about a person that is willing to philander is that they say they are cheating for different reasons. For example, the old excuse I have been given by a lot of philanderers. "The spark has gone out of our relationship." What that really means is they want a vacation from their everyday life. Here is another excuse that many women have given me about why they philander, "My spouse doesn't understand me." "He does not spend enough time with me or the family". People get real, it is not that their spouses do not understand them, it is that those well-developed taste buds for variety are now searching for a new flavor. Many of the men that I have spoken to have given me this excuse, "I'm a man, it's a man thing." No excuse just that reason, for them that is enough; the fact that it is in their nature to cheat. There are other reasons that I have heard from both men and women such as "he or she is always working." "I fell out of love with him or her." "He or she cheated on me first this is just payback." I could go on and on about the different reasons that I have been given for a person philandering, but if I did that this guide would never end.

There are a lot of men out there that have said to me that they have tried to figure out why their wives cheated. In that same vein I have a lot of women that say the same thing. They tried to figure out why their husbands cheated on them. I am going to answer that question for you right now. THEY WANTED TO! They saw a man or a woman somewhere that interested them, and they decided to explore. Stop beating yourself up about it. Stop sitting there day after day wondering if you could have been a better wife or husband. If you did something wrong. If you gained a few pounds and it turned him or her off. THEY WANTED TO! That is all it was, so you might as well get on with the business of living your life. I have a theory about the kind of people that want to have a relationship with a committed man or woman, and I have given these people a name, Satan's Sisters, and Beelzebub's Brothers. Satan has eight sisters and Beelzebub eight brothers. So, I would like to introduce you to Satan Sisters and Beelzebub's Brothers right now. These are the misters and mistresses that you will be philandering with.

Satan Sisters

Satan's Sister: Semi pro (One of the best women to cheat with, is almost never dangerous.)

I call her the perfect woman to cheat with because she is a strictly the already married man or woman type of woman. She is a modern-day courtesan. She only wants you on a temporary basis from time to time. She is happy to see you "come" and even happier to see you go. Semi Pro is the mistress that you will have to put a little money into, however. She is more interested in what you can do for her rather than what you can do too her. Her reasoning is that she has limited access and time with you so she might as well have unlimited access and time with your money. Telling a woman like this all about your problems with your spouse will not have her skirt rising like a flag in the wind, but a breeze from a wave of your wallet will. Another reason that this woman is the best of Satan's sisters to philander with is because she will be true blue to form and not change into one or more of Satan's other sisters. Even though she is the type of woman that will not ask about your other life, it is still a good practice to be cautious and not give too much information about your primary life. Semi Pro is not one of Satan sisters that you must train. She has been sleeping with married men or women for an exceptionally long time and she is incredibly good at it. She also can keep her mouth closed about her personal relationships with her friends. She does not need the validation of her girlfriends that she is a strong and independent woman because she already knows it. This is always an asset.

This woman often is attractive, has a great body and a good conversationalist. Another thing that you must expect of this sister is that she has her own rules, and she makes sure that you stick to them. For the most part you never have to wonder where this lady is coming from because she will always let you know. Remember that being a good and generous sugar daddy with this type of woman will get you what you want without any hassles. Another of her schools of thought is that she is the vacation from your primary life and like all good vacations you must pay for them.

The fact that she is getting what she wants out of the relationship (sex and money) keeps her happy and compliant.

Nothing in life is free. You will pay for your pleasures in one way or another, so why not do it to keep the hassle out of your other relationship. It will be up to the two of you to determine what that price will be.

Satan's Sister: Adventure (Good to Philander with but may be dangerous or fatal to your primary relationship.)

This sister is the "I will try anything once" type of woman. She is your second-best choice of women to cheat with. I say second best because she is out for an adventure in and out of bed. The motivating factor with this woman is that she is most likely getting out of or just out of an unsatisfying relationship. It may also be possible that she has not had a relationship in an awfully long time.

The good thing about this woman is that she is trainable or as I have heard men say, "you can run her." One of the reasons that this sister is trainable is because much of the time she is a younger woman and has not had the experiences of more mature Satan's sister. But you need to be careful with this sister because if you push too hard, she could become dangerous or even a fatal type of Satan's sister and then you have a problem.

This is where it pays off to be a gentleman. Treat her almost as you would treat a child with a gentle but firm hand. Do not give her too much attention or too little. You will know what to do from her reactions to the things you say and do. When she does not get what she wants she will see this as a rejection and that can be dangerous. Satan's Sister Adventurer has been known to do things like call her man's home at all hours. Show up at his work or even follow him around to check out his spouse.

Pillow talk can be dangerous with this one if she is really into you. So, it is always best to get her in hand and keep her in hand. Rules are a particularly good thing in order to train her and keep her in line.

Never lie to this sister or tell her anything that you are not prepared to back up or deliver on.

Most importantly remember to never give her much or any information about your primary life. Always talk to her in generalities when it comes to your primary relationship. Tell her what her place is always in your life and keep her there, never ever allow her to cross the lines that you have set for your relationship

Satan's Sister: Gullible
(Good to philander with, takes
a little work, is naive or stupid
and is trainable.)

This is another one of Satan's sisters that is a good candidate to cheat with because not only is she gullible, but she is also highly trainable. Sister Gullible is an easy woman and has many of the same qualities as Satan's sister Desperate, who we will review later in this guide. With this Mistress, money is not as important as time with you. She is into you and will put up with a lot just to be with you. In many cases this woman has a good career or job going for her. She is book smart but not street smart or man smart. This woman sympathizes with all the woes of your primary relationship, in her mind you need her, and she loves to be needed by you. She sees herself as your frequent vacation or haven from your primary life. The downside to a relationship with this woman is that she is often needy, and she takes a lot of work and effort. You must train this one well, if you are going to engage in minimal pillow talk with her. A big part of that training is always being honest with her. Like her sister Adventurer, you must always let her know what her place in Your life is always and keep her there. Also like her sister Desperate, she has not had a relationship in an exceedingly long time and wants that relationship badly.

The best way to achieve your goals with this sister is to use a firm and gentle hand. Small tokens of your affection on occasions are also affective in gaining her cooperation in your relationship. Flowers, candy and dinners on her birthday, drinks with her because she made you dinner etc., are a ten (10) in her book. Another thing to be cautious of with this sister is her advice-giving girlfriends.

She has without a doubt told them many of the aspects of your private relationship. It is a good idea to probe her every now and then about her friends. She is easily led by them so to know what her friends are telling her and the advice that they are giving her will work in your favor because it gives you an advantage in counteracting anything that they will tell her to do or say. However, remember to be incredibly careful about the subject of her friends. They are her safety net, her anchor, her sisters in the relationship struggle. It is not a good idea for you to attempt to break that bond.

Another advantage that you have in this situation is it gives you the appearance of caring about the other aspects of her life and her comfort level in it. You can lie to this woman and get away with it, but I would advise against it. It will be unnecessary to lie so why lie when you do not have to.

Satan's sister: Bitch
(Dangerous to philander with takes and lot of work. She can be controlled with the right skills. She could be fatal if handled the wrong way because she is the original tough cookie.)

This is an extremely dangerous woman to be involved with and she can and will be expensive. All that fire and passion that makes her such a good lover comes with a price. This sister believes with every fiber of her being that if your significant other gets a 2-carat diamond then she should get one as well. If the wife gets a cruise for two weeks, then she should get 2 weeks in Hawaii. Like sister Semi-Pro she feels that she deserves monetary gain. However, her belief stems more from the fact that it is a substitute for you. She agreed to be your Mistress, but she does not like it because she in into you and wants to be more in your life.

Pillow talk is a no-no with this woman. Be assured that it will be used against you should the relationship not go the way she wants it to. She is often looked upon by her girlfriends as a strong woman and at one time or another she attempted to mold her friends into her

31

own image unsuccessfully. This is because she often will befriend the sisters such as Gullible and Adventurer who are not as strong willed as she is. This sister can be had by the right man, however, It will require this man to take some of the "bitch" out of her. This can be accomplished in the following manner. Turn her into Satan sister Semi-Pro.

Sister Bitch is easier to deal with when she is Semi Pro, because now her focus becomes mostly monetary gain and sex rather than Anything else, such as building a permanent relationship with you. The way that you transform this woman is to take her in hand as soon as you realize she is being Satan's Sister Bitch. The first step you take is to let her come to you for advancement of the relationship or beginning the relationship. This becomes a subconscious bargaining point that she recognizes but will never acknowledge, because to do so puts her at a disadvantage. Begin by making sure Bitch understands that if a relationship between the two of you is to be conducted, then it must be done on your terms or not at all.

There are limits to everything so remember there is also a limit as to how many rules you will be allowed to set. Like most situations but especially when dealing with Bitch you must "pick your battles carefully". Give a little to get a lot. Whether or not you deal with Bitch as she herself or as Semi-Pro the money is not a point that she will allow you to negotiate too often, so this is not a battle that you can win all the time. Do bother to try however, it is a good idea to let her know how far your dollar will stretch. Put your foot down. The worst thing you can do is to allow this woman to dictate too many terms. Good sex and good times are great if that is what you're looking for, but you will have to get her to the same place if you want this to work. Bitch is many times frustrated because she cannot find a man that can deal with her and so in order to have her you must be that man.

Satan's Sister: Desperate
(Can be a good woman to philander with but can be dangerous or fatal to your primary life.)

This is the sister that must have a man in her life and will take any man that she can get. Someone else's man will do just fine. Satan Sister Desperate is in many ways like her sister Gullible. Desperate's motivations are the same as Gullible in that she does not like to be alone. However, with Desperate she does not want the company of her friends but the company of her bed partner. Her friends always know when she has a man in her life because they do not hear from her. She places all her focus on that man. This sister will be a nagger and a whiner even though she has been advised of the limitations of your relationship. You must handle her with a firm but none too gentle hand just as you would Satan sister Bitch. If you find that she is unwilling to accept the rules, you should walk away from the relationship. This should not be a problem for you if you are not too emotionally invested. If you are, however, then it will be harder. You will find yourself wanting to call her or be with her for that willing to please attitude that she displays with you because that is the thing you like most about her. In order to avoid all that and keep her as your mistress, you should conduct the relationship in the following manner.

Pillow talk is out of the question with this woman. She is not above using it against you if she is in her most "I'm Satan's Sister Desperate" frame of mind. To tell her about your other life is like adding gas to a flame, you will get burnt. Make the focus of the relationship about her. Let her talk to you as much as she wants to about her life. You will find that most of her conversation and focus is on keeping you and pleasing you. Keep her away from any telephone numbers or email addresses that are associated with your primary life. Because if you decide to walk away from the relationship she can and will contact your significant other and tell her all about your relationship with her. Bottom line with this woman is to start training her at the beginning of the relationship. Be honest with her about her role in your life but in a gentle way. Let her know where the line is drawn and never allow her to cross it even once. She will question you about your primary life to see if she is giving you the 20% you feel that you are not getting in your primary relationship. Talk to her in generalities and not in facts, never ever in facts. Give her enough to make her believe that she is the frequent and needed vacation that you want and need from your primary life.

Satan's sister: HO
(Can be good to philander with but be cautious she can turn into Satan Sister Bitch.)

This sister is a piece of work because she is a combination of all her sisters. She is like Semi-Pro because she prefers married men, but a single man or woman will do just fine. Her motivations are different because she needs a man not just once a man. She is like her sister Desperate because she is the type of woman that will call a man every hour on the hour just to see what he is doing. To her, the frequent calls keep her firmly planted in a man's or woman's mind and has them believing that they cannot live without her (head games). She is a very suspicious person because she is insecure about herself. Like her sister Desperate she is also a whiner and a nagger. The reason that men or women bother with her is the sex. In the sex Department she is just like her sister adventurer, she will try anything once. If she likes it she'll do it twice.

Often, she needs monetary gain that a man can provide because she has a dead-end job and has limited funds for various reasons. She has expensive tastes that she cannot afford on her own and is always on the prowl for Beelzebub's Brother Sugar Daddy. You can control this woman with a firm hand and even firmer rules. She will accept these rules providing they come with cash. Never engage in pillow talk with this woman because she is no dummy. She will tell you all about her life in hopes that you will tell her all about yours. DO NOT DO IT! Trust and believe me when I tell you that any information that you give her about your primary life will come back to bite you on the ass.

This sister is a half-step above prostitute. A Pro will tell you she is in it for the money and how much it will cost you, this is her job, and she will let you know it. Sister Ho on the other hand will tell you how much it will cost you, but she is with you because she wants you, and you only in her bed. There will always be a price for her favors, and she will make sure that you enjoy your time with her so that you look at the money as well spent and therefore you will be happy to pay the price.

This is another one of Satan sisters that is best handled by rules. Unbreakable rules. Make sure that she knows what her place in your life is always and keep her there. This is a relationship that you will have to put some money into, but you can limit the amount by letting her know upfront how much it is worth to you and that is all you are willing to pay. She will respect the fact that you were straight with her.

Satan's Sister: Slut
(She is alright to philander with but can be dangerous or fatal to your primary relationship. She comes with a warning label... "Handle with caution!")

This chick will sleep with any man anytime anywhere and anyplace, so getting sex from her will not be a problem. My grandmother would describe this woman as peanut butter (spread and ready). She wants what she wants, and she feels that good sex is the best way to get it. For the most part she is 20% Semi-Pro, 20% Bitch, 20% Ho and 40% a whole new kind of chick that adds up to 100% Alley Cat. This sister has no morals and no honor. She cannot and will not see past what she wants and what she wants is the only thing that matters. This woman always must be handled cautiously. Pillow top with this sister is like putting a loaded gun to your head and pulling the trigger. As with her other sisters she needs to be aware of her place in your life and she needs to understand that she will not be allowed across that line. So do not avoid any issues with this one. Put your foot down and keep it there. If she is unwilling to live with the conditions of your relationship then it is best that you walk away because no matter what you do, you will not be able to change her. She is who she is, and she does not want to change for you or any other man. If you choose to keep her however, I will suggest that you employ all the rules that you have laid down and do not slip. Above all else do not give this sister access to your primary life because she can and will find a way to use it to her advantage. This woman will also require monetary inducements to gain her cooperation in the relationship. She likes looking good on your dime.

Satan Sister: Realist
(The best of the lot to cheat with if she is interested enough. Almost never dangerous or fatal. Never a person that you can control.)

This is not normally the type of Satan sister that would get involved with a committed man or woman however, if you bring enough to the table and mind you that must be a whole lot, she may consider it. This sister must want you badly in order to have her step out of the "no committed men or women" placed she is in. She is the type that would most likely never disrupt your primary relationship because she has accepted the fact that she is screwing someone that is not her own. You cannot change this sister and it is best you do not try. She will walk away from you if you try to make her life become all about being with you. She will have no problems doing this and will not look back. She is very self-contained and proud. The best way to have her as a mistress is to accept what you get from her and be happy with it.

She will expect you to treat her well and feel that you should do things for her without her having to ask. Basically, she wants a husband without the papers. This woman is street smart as well as man smart and she will be blunt in letting you know it. Do not bother telling her all the woes of your primary relationship because she knows that if it were really that bad you would have been gone a long time ago. There are not many rules that you need to set with this woman such as not calling you or showing up or questioning you about your primary life because she already knows that this is not something she should do. However, if a non-attached person comes along and she finds that person interesting, she will drop you without a second thought.

Beelzebub's Brothers

Now that we have explored all the many facets of Satan's Sisters it is time to look at Beelzebub's Brothers. Ladies and interested parties, these are the men That you will be philandering with. They can be just as good or just as trifling as their sisters

Beelzebub's brother :
Natural Born Cheater
(Great man to philander with but can be dangerous or fatal to your primary relationship if he does not get what he wants.)

Natural Born Cheater is almost the perfect man to cheat with because he is the male version of Satan Sister Semi-Pro. The fact that he is good at cheating makes him want to cheat to improve his skills. This brother is into married women primarily but if a single woman can give him what he wants, that will work as well. Natural Born Cheater is the type of man who is part Beelzebub's Brothers Lady's Man and part brother Sugar Daddy. He does not mind putting money into a relationship if it gets him instant gratification but primarily feels that the person, he is screwing should finance their rolls in the hay as she or he most likely has a spouse's or significant other's income. NBC expects a big return on his investment if he puts up any cash. For example, if he buys you dinner and drinks, he will also be willing to pay for the hotel room if he gets sex all night long as many times in as many ways as he wants it. Also like his sister Semi-Pro you can tell him about the problems you have in your primary relationship, but he really does not care. The bottom line with NBC is that he enjoys fucking you and he wants to continue.

My grandmother always said, "a man's dick knows the skin, it does not know the face". In this case this man is a perfect example of that. Any woman that decides that this is the man she wants to philander with has made a good choice however, she must remember to do one important thing. Be straight with him always. Tell him what the limits are and make him understand that you will not go beyond them. He will respect that from you. It will not bother him that he is a friend with benefits in your life; In fact, he likes that aspect of the relationship. Let him know that he is a frequent and great vacation from your primary relationship, and you are willing to pay for it if need be. Also like his sister Semi-Pro, this is what he expects and will let you know it. Please be advised that this man has turned sex into an art form. He knows a lot about what women want in bed and has no problem letting you have it. He is sometimes married himself and has been caught philandering at least once. He is an intelligent person that learns from his mistakes in any situation and will employ that knowledge in the future.

Beelzebub's Brother:
Lady's Man (Good to philander with, almost never fatal to a primary relationship but can fall hard for the woman of his dreams and then he does become dangerous.)

Beelzebub's Brother Lady's Man is the type that just loves the ladies. Tall, short, fat, slim, eight to eighty blind cripple or crazy, he just loves the ladies. He fancies himself "the last of the great lovers".

He is often a handsome man, and he uses his good looks to his advantage. He is interesting to women because he knows a little about a lot of things and he has made it his life's work to know a great deal about women. Like Natural Born Cheater he is practiced in the art of sex, the seduction of women and employs that knowledge well. The difference between this man and Natural Born Cheater is that Beelzebub's brother Lady's Man tends to want more than what his mistress is willing to give. He likes to push the boundaries just to see what he can or cannot get away with. You can have a successful secondary relationship with this man if a woman is firm and controls his emotions thereby controlling his actions. Limited pillow talk is alright with this man but make the information general never specific. This is a man that you can have a meaningful conversation with but never anything specific about your primary life because that will come back to create problems for you. Have a good time with this man, encourage him to enjoy the relationship by your actions and your attitude when you are with him. Set the ground rules first with him and he will stick to them and have a good time within those boundaries.

Beelzebub's brother: Lover (Good to philander with, but use caution, he can be dangerous to your primary relationship when out of control.)

Ladies and others, if you are looking for a secondary relationship for great sex then you have gone to the right place with this brother. Beelzebub's Brother Lover is an expert at love making. Great sex is the thing that he uses as a hammer to beat a woman into submission. Having sex with this man can make a blind woman see, a sick woman well, and a crippled woman stand up and walk. He is a true sexual Dynamo, and he takes intimacy to a whole new level. He is the type of man that learns your body's rhythm so he can play it like a Stradivarius violin. When I instruct you to be cautious with this man it is because he has attributes of Lady's Man. He tends to want to push the boundaries and have more of your time and attention than you can allow. Here is where the caution comes in, just as with Beelzebub's Brother Lady's Man you must deal with him using a firm hand. Never allow him to get away with anything because the smallest thing he gets away with will encourage him to attempt to get away with bigger things. If this brother is in that new relationship haze, he will want to be with you as often as possible and then some. He is not above trying to contact you at the wrong times...i.e., when you are with your family, in order to coerce you into seeing him. The relationship is not feeding his heart but his ego. Lover cannot accept the fact that a woman that he has made love to does not want to be with him 24 hours a day, 7 days a week.

Like my grandma Mellie used to say, "baby girl ain't nothing worse than a man that thinks too highly of himself because that means he thinks nothing of you." Another aspect of lover's personality is that he loves that new relationship feeling, but he quickly loses interest, and then he is off in search of that feeling all over again. Do not fall for this man, he is not permanent relationship material he is a sexual bumblebee, and he wants to pollinate every flower that he can.

Beelzebub's brother: Pimp (Great to philander with but you will pay for the privilege.)

Beelzebub's Brother Pimp can be the total package of who to look for in a philandering partner. He knows what a woman wants in bed and is willing to give her all she can handle with the right motivation… money. He is great eye candy as he is often an extremely attractive man. He is like his brother Natural Born Cheater in some ways because he knows the rules of the relationship and is willing to play by them when he wants to. Pimp is the type that invites an open relationship. He wants to know the rules and if you do not bring up the subject then he will. This man is the closest male version of his sister Semi-Pro because he also believes in time with your money rather than time with you. He loves receiving gifts from his lady friends and has no problem making suggestions on what to get him. In fact, this brother will come right out and let you know the cost of his favors.

Another thing that you need to be aware of with this brother is that he has an excessively large ego. If he makes you scream and wither in bed, he feels that he has earned his pay, and it puts another notch in his sexual bedpost. As with his sister Semi-Pro the way you want to handle him is to let him know what your price range is and do not make exceptions for him. He will always have a problem that you need to solve. He will expect you to be his financial safety net to solve all his financial problems. It would be best for you if you did not, because Pimp is the original "give an inch but take a mile man".

Beelzebub's brother: Kissing Cousin (Good to philander with but he will allow himself to be sucked into your primary relationship.)

Kissing cousin takes a laid-back approach towards a secondary relationship as a rule. Women tend to try and figure this man out and that always leads to problems especially when there is nothing to figure out. He is who he is an women involved with this man need to take him with a grain of salt. Kissing cousin is never the same man twice he is just a go with the flow type of guy and is good at adjusting to fit the situation. This brother only becomes a problem when you pull him into your primary life. One minute he has that laid back attitude about things and the next he is advising you on the way to conduct your primary relationship. In most cases this man is not in love he is in lust. Just like Beelzebub's brother Lover, he has found a woman that he enjoys the sex act with, and he wants to continue.

You will never get pressure or a hassle from him if you do not pull him into your primary life. If you do, he will become "Captain Save a Ho" then he will proceed to turn your world upside down with his belief that he knows what is best for you. Kissing Cousin is an easy guy to fall for because he makes you feel that you can tell him all your problems and no matter what the situation is he will always be on your side. If he is not emotionally invested in you and has maintained his laid-back attitude, then the relationship can and will be very enjoyable. If or when he falls for a woman, he will fall hard and that can be a problem if he knows too much about your primary life.

He is not above using what he knows about your life if he feels that it will make you do as he wishes or leave your primary life for him. The way to handle this brother is to not bring him into your primary life at all. Talk to him in general terms and always keep the ground rules in play. It will be exceedingly difficult to do this because the brother can be an overly sweet, loving, and attentive man, and therefore Mistresses tend to fall for him. You must keep him out of your primary life if you intend to keep your primary relationship intact.

Beelzebub's brother: Player (Can be good to philander with but be careful he can be fatal to your primary life.)

This man is the worst of the brothers to get involved with because normally he has no conscience, he is as morally bankrupt and dishonest as his sister Slut, and he is proud of that fact. This man cares only for himself. To him women are notches on his belt and nothing more. This is one of the reasons that he is so appealing to women, because he is a true bad boy.

The player would have no problem leaving messages on your home phone or using pillow talk information in order to get what he wants. The only woman that can deal with him is Semi Pro because she has no aspirations of a long-term relationship with him. Like him she is out for what she wants from him and in no way is she interested in keeping him. He is interchangeable to her and her favorite word to him would be "next". If any other of Satan sisters attempts to be with him, it is advisable to keep him on a noticeably short leash. Tell him absolutely nothing of your primary life and make it clear from the onset that he is a bootie call and nothing more.

Praise his sexual prowess and make him proud and satisfied with that as a basis for your relationship. The more you control this relationship in the beginning the less you will have to control it in the later stages. Do not put any emotional funds into this man because you will not get a good return on your investment. Player is not in it for the money as much as he is in it for the glory of his friends. Trust me when I tell you that every aspect of your relationship has been bandied about by him and his friends.

You will never be the only mistress he will have at one time. He will have many and have them often. For you, keeping a steady supply of condoms should be a constant practice to prevent you going home with something that you did not leave with. Like my grandma you used to say "never let what's between his legs rule what's in your head. You are bound to mess them both up."

Beelzebub's brother: Sugar Daddy (Excellent to philander with but understand that he wants a lot of time for his money.)

This Gent is a combination of old school player and lover. He has heard it all and done even more. He has not just been around the block; he built a part of that block. This one is not easily fooled however frequent sex keeps his mind occupied and you may be able to get some things past him.

Beelzebub's Brother Sugar Daddy is often married, and his mate is no longer or very seldom interested in sex. He figures that is what you are for, so he does not bother her for it. Sugar Daddy is looking to sow those last few wild oats left in the barrel with a firm body and a tight ass. He respects your straightforwardness, and he likes to know what he can do with you, how often and where because he is an uncomplicated man.

A small amount of pillow talk will not hurt with this one but be careful because he will seize any opportunity to control as much of your life as possible. He will always want younger women in his life for that reason because they are easy to control, and he can teach them many things about life men and relationships. Like my grandma used to always say "old dogs like fresh meat to".

Sugar Daddy has no problem opening his wallet for his Mistress, but he lets you know that there are limits to his financial assistance. This is the type of man that can have a secondary relationship with you that is fulfilling and good.

Sugar Daddy is the type of man that is the male version of my grandmother. He is incredibly wise when it comes to human nature, and he is often the best person to seek advice from. There is not a whole lot of prep work that you need to do with this man. Unlike his brothers he knows what he wants, and he does not want a lot of hassle getting it. He wants a vacation from his normal life and if you're a good vacation then he will continue to take you and pay for you.

Beelzebub's brother: SAP (A poor choice in a philandering partner. He is more trouble than he is worth.)

He is the saddest and most useless of all of Beelzebub's brothers. This man is a hot mess, a whiner, a nagger, and is exceedingly needy. He is his sister Desperate intensified. He falls in love with every woman that he meets and then proceeds to drag them down with him. Often this man comes with a heavy load, and he wants a woman that can help him carry that baggage.

Never take part in pillow talk with this man because he will use it all to manipulate you or even threaten you to do what he wants. Give this man only one way to contact you and one way only. Your best option would be an answering service or an additional cell phone. Never give him any information about your primary life. He will ask you about it all the time but be firm with him and let him know that there is a line that he will never be allowed to cross, and your other life is that line. Make Sap understand that it is your way or the highway. When he feels that he has no other choice which is often the situation in his mind, he will do things to put your primary life in jeopardy. Sap would be more than willing to show up at your door or call your house if he has this information because nothing is off limits to him.

In reality this man does not have a great personality and he comes across to most people as arrogant, there for most people don't want to be around him, but Sap can be charming when it suits his purpose. That is his hook. When you first meet him, he comes off like a great guy because he talks a good game, but he soon becomes a nightmare. That is when you see his true colors. Not all at one time mind you but over a period. I would estimate within 3 to 6 months.

In a relationship with this man what you do not know will hurt you. He is the worn-out wolf in sheep's clothing. He has been worn out by all the mess that he has gotten himself into and has no idea how to get out of his mess. For the most part he is below average intelligence, but his sappy smile and somewhat boyish ways attract women, some find it endearing. When you recognize this man for what he is even though it is late in the game put him in his place. If he wants more and you are not prepared to give more, do not walk away from this man RUN! This is most definitely the kind of brother that you want to feed with a long handle spoon. If the sex is that good and you want to keep this brother, be always on your toes.

PART 2
The Match Making Game

I have said it once, and I will say it again…. "Look in the bed before you get in it, that way you know who or what you are dealing with." I also want to tell you something that I heard my grandfather say once and it is so appropriate when it comes to philandering. "Hunting ain't no fun when the rabbit got the gun." For the country wisdom impaired that means that cheating is great until you are dealing with the wrong person. To that end I would like to give you some examples of good matches among Satan's Sisters and Beelzebub's Brothers.

Say Satan sister Semi- Pro and Beelzebub's brother Lover and Sugar Daddy.

Satan sister Adventurer and Beelzebub's brothers Sugar Daddy and Pimp.

Satan sister Gullible and Lady's Man and Sugar Daddy.

Satan sister Bitch and Beelzebub's brothers Natural Born Cheater, Lady's Man, and Lover.

Satan sister Desperate and Beelzebub's brothers SAP (be careful) and Kissing Cousin.

Satan sister Ho and Beelzebub's brothers Player and Sugar Daddy.

Satan sister Slut and Beelzebub's brothers Lady's Man, Natural Born Cheater and SAP (again be careful).

Satan sister Realist and Beelzebub's brothers Lover, Kissing Cousin, and Sugar Daddy

PART 3
Telephone an E-Mail
(The Deadly Duo)

The tell tales telephone, that is what I call it because the telephone will tell tales of all it knows just by revealing a few numbers. Now this is for the straight up stupid... If you think that your spouse is not checking your personal communication equipment, please think again. They have been, are currently, and will forevermore continue to check and see who you are talking to. The following stories are just a few examples of real people who have been done in by the deadly relationship killer called the telephone:

Lesson 1: Never give your Mister or Mistress your home, work or cellular telephone number. It is a good idea to get a separate cell phone.

David C.: David C. had the bright idea to give his mistress his home telephone number with strict instructions that she was only to use it during certain hours of the weekday and never on the weekends. Does this sound like a good plan to you? Well, his mistress

Satan Sister Bitch did not think so. She called old David at all the prohibited times and would hang up every time his wife answered. Now I am sure that all the growling whispers of "I told you not to call me now!" Did not help matters at all. The hang up calls were just the straws that broke the camel's back. In the end old David's loving wife decided to follow him one night after one too many of those hang-up calls when he said he was going out with the boys. She followed him straight to a meeting with his mistress.

David C. Is now divorced and living in a one-bedroom apartment on the Southside of Chicago.
WHAT HE SHOULD HAVE DONE: David should have begun by making sure Bitch understood that if a relationship between the two of them was to be conducted it must be on his terms or not at all. David C. should have never engaged in pillow talk with his mistress because it gave her a weapon that she could and did use against him. He should have given a little to get a lot. As in good sex a little time and a little cash. He also should have had a separate phone for her.

Paula J.: Like David C. Paula thought that giving her Mister only her cell number was a brilliant idea. Well, that turned out to be just the opposite. Dear sweet wife Paula was in the car with her spouse when she received a call from her Mister who just called to see what she was doing. Paula, not knowing what to do, tried to pretend that it was a call from a work colleague. Now hubby was a smart man and quickly figured out that this was no business call. At his earliest opportunity hubby checked the calls on his wife's cell phone and called all the numbers back pretending to be a floral delivery driver. As you can imagine, Paula is now a divorcee and spending a great deal of her time having drinks with her girlfriends while whining about the fact that her ex-husband has a new wife that is younger than she is and pissed that she is thinner too.

WHAT SHE SHOULD HAVE DONE: Limited pillow talks with her Mister but make the information general and never specific. Kept him happy when they were together, in bed and out, that would have distracted him away from your primary life. She should have set the ground rules first with him and he would have stuck to them and had a good time within those boundaries. When she realized that the man was going to be a problem, she should have put him in his place.

If the sex was that good then she should have kept him, but she should have been always on her toes. Last and certainly not least, she should not have allowed him access to contact information.

Mary L.: Mary L. was a successful small business owner, and you would think that she would have been smarter about her philandering but like some many others she was overcome by the power of the prick. Desperately needing to hear her mister's voice as often as possible, Mary L. gave her mister her home telephone number along with instructions that he was only to call during certain hours of the day and never at night. Well, it just so happened that her mister did follow her instructions, but she should have instructed him a little further by telling him never to leave a message for her on her machine. Mary is not divorced but you can best believe that she is on lockdown like an inmate during a prison riot. Mary L. has friends she has not seen in years.

WHAT SHE SHOULD HAVE DONE: Mary L. should have gotten a cell phone that her spouse did not know about and an answering service that would have sent messages for her. I will say it again, your mister or mistress is a vacation from your everyday life. PAY FOR IT!

In this modern age of computerized communication, one of the many deadly components is enabling email. The email will enable your soon to be ex-spouse to take every dime out of your pocket faster than you can say "defended". The email is the worst thing to happen to the philanderer since the invention of the divorce lawyer. Here are just some of the many examples of the enabling email.

Lesson 2: Never send your mister or mistress an email from your personal or professional email address.

Sally P.: Sally was a woman on the way up and had many things that she had worked extremely hard to get. One of the things that she wanted most was a sweet thing on the side for those times that she needed to get away from the pressures of her primary life. Sally decided that she would take up the offer of a tall drink of water from the office next door and you know "live a little". Sally, in her infinite wisdom decided to email her Mister all the naughty things that she wanted to do with him on their first date. Sally's mistake was that she decided to send this email from her PC at her residence. Not two days later Sally P.'s spouse found the email from his faithless spouse. Not only did he read the email, but he sent copies of the email to all their family and friends to read so that he would have plenty of witnesses in the divorce proceedings. Sally isn't married anymore, and that tall and good-looking drink of water is not so good-looking anymore.

Tommy J.: Tommy was your classic lady's man, smooth talker, good looking and great in bed. Tommy met Shirley in a bar one night and decided that this was the perfect woman to have a hot and heavy affair with. Tommy being the man that he was also decided that he could carry on the affair via email, but what Tommy did not think of was the fact that just putting an email in the trash is not enough, you must dump the trash.

What Tommy also neglected to take into consideration was the fact that his wife of four months was not as trusting and ignorant as he had hoped. So, when his dear wife was scouring the email looking for one, she discarded, she found all the emails that had been sent to her spouse's mistress. Having had her illusion shattered that her spouse was a loyal and loving husband and soon to be father, Tommy's wife left her spouse and took with her a great portion of his income in alimony and child support.

Beth B.: Beth B. was a good wife and mother who was married to a not so good spouse, that we will call Mike B. Now not only was Mike a bad spouse but he was also a stupid philanderer. Beth B went about her daily life being that good wife to Mike, when low and behold one day she found an email message not sent to her but to Mike requesting he give his mistress a call because she had not seen him for days and she was oh so lonely without him. Beth got the house, the car, alimony, and the satisfaction knowing that Mike now lives with his parents in their basement while listening to daily lectures on "the bad turn his life has taken".

PART 4
Lies: Who to tell, when to tell, what to tell.

When it comes to being honest, things are simple. Never be honest with your spouse and if you are philandering, always be honest with your mister or mistress.

The object is not to complicate any of your lives. So, you do not want to tell too many lies that you will need to keep track of later. One thing you should never do is lie to your mister or mistress because they are the secondary life, and they should know it. So, there is no need to lie to them.

Always being honest with your mister or mistress gives them a clear picture of where they stand and lets them know that they cannot go beyond the boundaries that have been set in your relationship. This takes the hassle out of cheating.

Your mister or mistress will have no choice but to go with the flow or get out of the game. On the other hand, lying to your spouses is necessary to maintain your primary life. What is tricky about this situation is that philanderers tend to tell more lies than are needed, or they will do things that are not necessary, and it will cause them to tell even more lies. Husbands and wives have an almost six cents about a spouse's philandering and the more reason you give them to look, the more they will look and ask questions.

When you lie to your spouse try and stick as close to the truth as possible. Do not embellish the lie or get too many others involved because your spouse can check with them for verification. Like my grandma used to say, "lying is like branches on a tree baby girl, the more you put fertilizer on them the bigger the branches are going to get". A prime example of a bad lie to tell your spouse is the old tried and failed excuse "I'm going to hang with the boys". That lie will get you caught every time. This advice is not just for men but women as well. All that needs to happen is for your spouse to bump into one of the boys or one of the girls and casually ask about your evening out and you are caught faster than you can say "baby let me explain". Another good rule of thumb to live by when you are philandering is to always have some sort of evidence to back up the lie. An example of this would be I was working late leave a preplan note out where your spouse can easily see it meet with client X reference merger or Thursday at 7:00 PM. Put that note in your day planner for example, it is a good idea to have this note visible prior to the date that you plan to be living your secondary life. If you think your spouse has not seen the note leave the day planner at home and open to that page, then call home and ask if you left your day planner.

PART 5
Time Management

When you are scheduling time with your secondary life it is never a good idea to try and cram time into your day to see your mister or mistress. This situation causes you to come up with a place you need to be at the last minute and that can get you into trouble. To combat this issue be prepared for events in your secondary life. Never make plans at the last minute with your mister or mistress. Set a schedule and stick to it as closely as possible.

You may be thinking that a routine may make a spouse question for example, where you go every Friday from 8:00 to 10:00 PM. You are correct in thinking this. A routine such as this is a sure-fire way to cast suspicion on yourself. The best way to set a schedule is to set it around your spouse's schedule. For example, if your spouse works late on Friday, then that is an opportunity to spend time with your secondary life. Please note that no plan is foolproof, so be careful. Just because a spouse has a schedule, things change, and shit happens.

PART 6
Philandering Indicators

There are signs of philandering that people give off when they have or are engaging in a secondary life. Often the partner notices these signs. It is always a good idea to check yourself. Be aware of the way you are acting, and make sure that it is not out of character for you. If you think that you have your spouse fooled and that you're acting out of character has gone unnoticed, please think again. Nothing may be said at the time but trust and believe that now they are watching you a bit closer.

Let us look at some of the other philandering indicators that have gotten philanderers caught:

1. Lipstick or makeup on your shirt.
I know that many men think that this is an obvious one that every man with a brain should know. You would be surprised how many times men have been caught cheating because of a cosmetic blunder. Gentlemen check yourself before you go home.

2. Hang up calls at your home.

If your spouse keeps getting hang up calls at your home and it has never happened before, he or she will get suspicious. Earlier in this guide I advised you to never allow your mister or mistress to have access to your home phone number, this is the reason why.

3. Change in attire.

A sudden change in your appearance is always an indicator that you have a reason for the change and if the reason is not bringing more income into your home, then your spouse will suspect that it is about sex. A person that lives in their sweatpants or that housedress does not suddenly start wearing slacks and skirts suits.

4. More attention to your appearance.

This goes hand in hand with number 3. Ladies, if you never wear makeup or take the time to choose your attire the night before you go to work, then when you start to do these things, that is a signal to your spouse that you have someone to look good for. Men that are not in the habit of shaving daily or are not overly concern about their clothes beyond the fact that they are clean do not suddenly do a 180 and become meticulous about everything that they wear down to the socks on their feet. It is a dead giveaway that you have a reason to change your appearance.

5. More late hours at the office.

If you are one of those employees that starts the

countdown to leave work 30 minutes before quitting time and suddenly, you're working late two and three nights a week, trust and believe that your spouse suspects that you are philandering.

6. liking things you hated before.
If your spouse has been trying to get you to go to a museum or the opera and suddenly you become a patron of the arts or a theater buff. Trust me when I tell you, your spouse knows that you are cheating.

7. Criticizing things that you did not care about before.
If your spouse had a filthy mouth when you met them and was vocal about their opinions and you never had a problem with it before, do not have a problem with it after you start cheating. Be aware that your mister or mistress will wonder why the sudden change you your opinion of them.

8. Excuses for leaving the house more often (including starting arguments).
Slick, if you think that you are picking fights with your spouse and then storming out of the house at all hours has gone unnoticed, please think again. Your spouse has noticed, and he or she may not say anything at the time, but they are watching.

9. Paying less attention to your spouse.
Partner, paying less attention to your spouse is not the thing to do when you are having an affair. Your best

bet is to pay more attention to your spouse when you come home and pay attention to the little things. If she changes her shade of lipstick, compliment her. If he or she gets his or her haircut in a different style pay attention and give an opinion good or bad.

10. Coming home smelling different. (Fresh from the shower, close freshly washed or smelling of perfume or Cologne).
If you get caught because of this, then you are a stupid philanderer and you deserve what you get. Baby wipes work wonders on your private parts. Buy some and leave them at your mister or mistress' place.

11. Hanging out with the guys or the girls more often.
If it is normal for you to hang out with the guys or the girls a couple of times a week do not change your routine, you can always make time to see your mister or mistress once a week or more when your spouse has a meeting or must work late.

12. Underwear found in the car.
If you are making out in the car then you need to be caught. Do not be cheap get a hotel room and have your mister or mistress meet you there.

13. Receipts and card statements for gifts and flowers your spouse did not get.
Dummy, pay cash and toss the receipt. It is a good idea to put some cash away for occasions that you need to buy a gift for your Mister or mistress.

14. Suddenly having a lock or code on your cell phone that your spouse does not know.

If you have always had a code on your cell, then you are good to go. If you have never had a lock or code on your cell, then it is a good idea to get a second cell that your spouse does not know about. Make sure that you pay for the cell phone in cash.

15. Change in sexual habits. (All of a sudden you like it kinky).

If you have a mister or mistress, you have them for what you do not get at home. Do not bring your kink home if it was not there before. If your spouse wants something new or different, they will let you know.

16. Tell lies that do not make sense or are unnecessary. It is better to limit your answers than to tell lies that do not make sense or are unnecessary because your spouse will see right through them.

Does My Spouse Suspect?

I wrote this section of the manuscript because I wanted my readers to think. Nothing that you do is 100% foolproof or effective because some spouses just have suspicious minds. You could be the most innocent person in the world and the suspicious minded will still suspect you of wrongdoing. In those situations that is something that one will just have to deal with if you want to retain your primary relationship.

Spouses who suspect their mates of cheating can be more cunning than the philanderer themselves. Short of flat out asking your spouse if he or she suspects you of philandering, you may never know until you have been caught. Therefore, I advise you to be always vigilant. Do not maneuver yourself into a trap of your own making. You know your spouse as well as anyone ever could, so my advice to you is to look for the warning signs.

The following are a few signs from your spouse that they may suspect you of philandering:

1. When your spouse questioned your activities more than usual.

2. When your spouse makes smart aleck comments about your activities that indicate he or she thinks you are lying about your whereabouts.

3. When your spouse checks your communication devices, this includes your cell phone, Facebook page and any other communication device that you have.

4. When your spouse questioned why the position of the seat in your vehicle has moved or adjusted. When your spouse must question something that normally would not be considered noteworthy then be on high alert you are under suspicion.

5. When your spouse drops by your place of employment unexpectedly and often.

6. When your spouse questions your friends and family about group activities. This is the reason that I advised you earlier in this manual to not involve friends or family in your philandering.

7. Some spouses will be so bold as to smell their mates when they arrive home.

Just a general note: if you have been caught philandering before, you are always under suspicion of cheating. It is the price you pay for cheating and being caught.

PART 7
Things You Should Never Do

The things that I am about to tell you may seem like common knowledge, but you would be amazed how many people make these common errors in judgment that never fail to get them caught while philandering.

Never have an affair with a close friend of your spouse. The reason for this is simple, most affairs end and many of them end badly.

If this relationship ends badly. Your Mister or mistress. Will go to your spouse with all the details of your failed relationship.

The two things that never work out well. Sex tapes and threesomes. These two things are bad ideas on so many levels, the least of which being. You are leaving evidence of your philandering.

Never sleep with a relative of your significant other. This goes along with number one never having an affair with a close friend. Sleeping with a relative of your spouse is even worse.

Never take pictures with your Mister or mistress. If that relationship ends badly, those pictures will be used against you. They will show up on your ex-mister or mistresses Facebook page, Twitter, Instagram, and other sights that you most likely have not even heard of before. Trust me when I tell you that people that declared their undying love to you will give your spouse a reason to kill you, while your mister or mistress loves you right into the grave.

Never drive your mistress or mister's car, and never allowed them to drive yours. You do not want to have to come up with a story to explain to your friends and or your spouse why you were driving a different car or why someone else was driving your car. Your automobile is very familiar to your friends and family. A simple denial that you were not driving a different car will never work because many times it may not be just the car, but what is in or on the car. A dent in the passenger side door. Or the custom wheels? Or the cute little magnet or sticker that's on your car that every one of your friends and family is familiar with. Don't do it, save yourself the hassle.

Never take off your wedding ring: first, your mister or mistress already know that you're married, so there's no need to remove your wedding ring when you are with them. Secondly, you will forget to put it back on sooner or later, and that will only serve to make your spouse suspicious. No matter what excuse you come up with, your spouse is not going to believe that's the reason you took off your wedding band.

If you decide to take a day off work to play hooky with your mister or mistress, make sure that you have arranged a cover story such as a conference, training, or a seminar.

Purchase unscented wipes and leave them at your mister or mistress' place. They have no scent so you will not come home as if you just stepped out of the shower or smelling like you just had sex.

Get used to calling your spouse and you mister or mistress "babe". It is inevitable that you will sooner or later call your spouse by your mister or mistress' name and that will cause you to seek and new residence.

Never and I do mean never ever have unprotected sex with your Mr. or mistresses. Purchase condoms, lots, and lots of condoms. Use them always never ever assume or believe that your Mr. or mistress will take care of contraception. You do not want to go home carrying something you did not leave with. Preventing pregnancy is not the only reason for wearing a condom.

Forward the philanderer with children, never communicate with your Mr. or mistress within earshot of your children.

You can put money on the fact that they will run straight to mom or dad to tell them all about the pretty lady or the funny man that mom or dad was making funny eyes at today.

A lesson in geography; never take your Mr. or mistress to the same restaurants and bars that you take your spouse, people know you there.

Don't be cheap. Having a Mr. Or mistress is like taking frequent vacations from your everyday life and like any good vacation you have to pay for them.

Never admit to an affair after it is over. If you had an affair and it is over that is a secret that you should take with you to your grave. I once had a friend that admitted to her spouse that she had a brief affair with another man. She told me that she informed her spouse because she felt guilty about what she had done.

Hell no! Put it out of your mind and move on with your married life. There is nothing to be gained by coming clean afterwards. If you don't listen to anything else that I tell you in this manual listen to this….. your spouse is going to have one of three reactions to your admission:

1: Your spouse will say that they forgive you and then set about treating you badly. They will expect you to accept this bad treatment because of your admission of philandering and that you should expect such treatment because you deserve it. No matter what your spouse does, his or her justification will be that you cheated.

2: Your spouse will leave the house or demand that you leave the house and then file for divorce.

3: Your spouse will forgive you and want to move past your philandering. Even though your spouse will mean this they will never again completely trust you and they will never see you in the same way that they did before.

PART 8
Matters of the Heart

When it comes to matters of the heart, there is only what happened before your heart was broken and what happened after your heart was broken. It's like a mark in time, nothing is the same again and you will never see your spouse the same way you did before. You don't even look at men and women the same way either.

I surmise that this is one of the reasons why some people think of philandering. To either dull the pain or get payback against their partner for the betrayal. After all, Satan's sisters and Beelzebub's brothers are everyday people just like you and me. There is nothing that sets them apart from one another other than the fact that they have chosen to be philanderers.

Grandmother used to say… "baby girl, your head will hold on to anything your heart tells it to". In translation that means if you keep telling yourself that you want a person that you are in love with that person for whatever reason you say, then you will believe that you are in love with that person.

More often than not this applies to women more than men. Often men will fight against what they feel rather than give into it. They believe in the adage…. "The best way to get over a woman is to get on top of another one".

Love is a powerful addiction, even the illusion of love has a powerful hold on a person's emotions. Just think for a minute of how many people you know that have had their lives changed by love and how many have had their lives turned upside down by the illusion of love.

That illusion is oh so much more powerful when you are in it alone. Men see love differently than women. Men are better about controlling their emotions when it comes to love. Women see that quality in men as being unfeeling or uncaring when it comes to matters of the heart.

There is a piece of advice that I would give to women, stop trying to make a man into what you want him to be. If he wasn't the man that he is you wouldn't have been attracted to him. The first thing that a woman should understand about men is that they are not you, men are never going to be you and therefore they are not going to react the way that you do when it comes to matters of the heart.

Many women feel that if they mother a man and take care of all their needs that man will be her prize. I want women to understand that being a good woman will not keep a man. Having a man's child or children will not keep a man. Being his maid, lover, chief cook, and bottle washer will not keep a man. The only way to keep a man is if that man wants to be kept by you. So, ladies stop treating a grown man as if he has no self-control.

There are only 2 things that do not have self-control… puppies and babies. This is one of the main subliminal messages that a man sends out to a woman. The dog whistles are….” It just happened.” “We are not exclusive.” “You don't pay me enough attention.”

A man needs to understand that his woman is not him, they are never going to be him so therefore, they are not going to be more emotional about love. The same reasons that I listed above are the main reasons that you just cannot understand why a woman makes a big deal over a man's philandering. If you go into any relationship thinking that you are going to change a person into what you want them to be or harness of woman's emotions, then you are headed for a long drop off a very deep Cliff. Women are messy emotional creatures. We create problems where there are none. We will lie, cheat, steal or even now and then commit murder to get what we want, when it comes to love or the illusion of love.

When it comes to matters of the heart, we really do believe that all is fair in love and war. It is unfortunate that men and women don't seem to understand that taking the stripes off a zebra will not make him a thoroughbred, it just makes him a stripe less zebra. What that means is whatever a person is when you meet them that's what they are always going to be. The things that a person must do, be it in your primary or secondary relationship, you must see what you're getting and either accept it for what it is or keep looking for what you want. Like my grandmother used to say…, "baby girl, if you don't want a stray dog at your door then don't feed it".

My dear grandmother said to me once…, "baby girl, don't never ask a man where he's going or where he's been because he just might tell you".

I believe I never understood that until many years later when a friend of mine told me that she questioned her spouse about his activities one night and he told her straight out that he had been with his longtime mistress at a party. She was devastated because all the signs were there, but she refused to see them. All her friends including me knew about the mistress and had told her, but she didn't listen to any of us. This is a prime example of holding onto what you really do not have.

A note about sex and the young:

Cultivating a relationship with a much younger person is commonplace today. If you are going to do this then you need to know why the younger person is willing to be in that relationship with you. Young women have sized up a potential partner financially. She wants your house, your car, and your money. She has sized you up and found you financially acceptable. She wants to be able to buy all the things that makes her happy on your dime. She is Semi Pro in training.

For a young man, he has done the exact same thing. He has sized up an older woman not only financially but her capacity to nurture and take care of him and he has found her acceptable.

In both these cases the main objective is to remain in a state of no responsibility for their life. They are substituting their parent(s) for you.

I want you to know what you're getting and why you're getting it.

Part 9
Quit Bitching and Whining

Alright people straight talk, I'm going to give you the real deal. You have been living on another planet when it comes to your primary relationship. You have been whining about him or her being a philanderer, bitching and moaning about him or her and praying that you will get through to them. Well now I am going to tell you what your family and friends are thinking but will never tell you to your face.

Let's start with the ladies: the first thing women need to remember is that you knew who they were and what they were like when you got with them. You have one of two choices: 1. You can leave and find a man or woman that will be and do what you want them to be and do. One of my favorite chestnuts is…, "If you don't like what you're getting, go find it somewhere else." Or 2. Stay in whatever relationship(s) that you have, quit bitching and whining and make peace with things as they are.

One of the most diluted statements that has ever been uttered by a scorned woman is "I just need some closure". You don't need closure, that is an excuse to continue to have continued connection with your ex-significant other. Closure is what you got when you got confirmation that he or she was philandering.

Your spouse did what they did because he or she wanted to. Move on with your life and go find what or who you want.

Now if you think that what I'm telling you is cold and unfeeling you will be wanting to hear the second option…., Suck it up! Stop bitching and whining, learn to enjoy the fringe benefits of being in a primary relationship with the philanderer and deal with the relationship as the situation stands. You are not going to change a man or a woman that doesn't want to be changed, and you are damn sure not going to appeal to his or her feelings for you as an anvil to anchor him or her to the relationship that you have firmly planted in only your mind. If you are not getting it like you want it, I suggest you start getting it elsewhere.

You see ladies, relationships are not actually hard, women in general tend to make them that way. Now there are exceptions to every rule and there are a few women out there that have learned to adapt to their situation or choose the best option for them. But, for the most part the latter is true. In one way or another every woman has an aspect or aspects of one of more of Satan sisters in them. Combine that with a woman's natural need to nurture and you have the perfect recipe for unhappiness and malcontent with any of Beelzebub's brothers.

In this day and age many people are of the opinion that women are more evolved than their counterparts of the 60s, 70s and 80s, but I say no matter how much things change the more they stay the same. Most women are still slaves to their feelings and to the need for that white picket fence with that perfect man or woman that will mow the lawn, rub their feet, kiss their brow, and take care of them until the day they die. They may have found new and inventive ways to get it, but it's all the same game they have just added some new players. So, lie to your family, lie to your friends but do not lie to yourself, you want what you want, and you will use anything at your disposal to get it. Just keep in mind that what you get may not be worth the work it took to get it. Now to the men, this is going to be short and sweet.

If a man is having problems with his primary relationship, it is normally due to money sex or time and many cases are a combination of all three. Now add that to your significant others' emotions and there is your recipe for unhappiness and malcontent. Every man for the most part likes sleeping with their significant other but all men and I do mean all men wish to be sleeping with a perfect female version of themselves. I have heard men say more than once that they want a "traditional woman" and a marriage like their parents had. Women do not have a problem being a "traditional woman", but they will only do so for a "traditional man". Meaning if you want to marry a woman like your mamma, then you must be like your daddy. That means that if you want a chick on the side then you must take care of home and keep your wife happy first. You cannot treat your home and your wife as unimportant playthings and expect her to be a traditional woman. That old chestnut of happy life when you have a happy wife is 100% true.

You men have the same choices as women do. 1 you can leave him or her and find someone to screw that is just like you or your option 2 is the same as the ladies. Quit bitching and whining. Understand that your significant other is exactly who they are. They have always been that way and they will always be that way. So, if you don't want to leave shut up. Suck it up and deal with the situation of your primary relationship as the situation stands. Just like women, every man has an aspect or aspects of Beelzebub's brothers in them, and they tell themselves the same lies that Satan's sisters tell themselves to justify their philandering. I have said it before, and I will say it again; you cheat because you want to. There is not a cheating gene out there that is passed from father to son. I will sing this song again; lie to your family, lie to your friends, but do not lie to the man in the mirror.

You want what you want, and you will use every method at your disposal to obtain it. For both men and women, the problem with lying to yourself is that in doing so you will do things that will get you into trouble in an effort to firmly cement the lie in your own mind. For example, if you find this man or woman in your office attractive and you have been flirting with this person. You have imagined that person in bed and all the things that you could do together and now you are saying to yourself, "I'm not cheating so it's OK to call this man or this woman from my home or mobile phone because this is just a friend". "It doesn't matter if my spouse sees the number because I'm not doing anything wrong". Liar! Because sooner or later if you have not already you are going to sleep with that person and at that moment you have become a philanderer and you have already put your primary relationship in jeopardy because your spouse suspects you of cheating just because of all the phone calls to that person. Here's another example for you to Mull over. "it's ok to have a drink with a person and not tell my spouse about it. It is perfectly innocent even if I'm planning to rip the clothes off this person at the first opportunity I get. Trust and believe me when I tell you that the other person in this little tryst is thinking the same thing and he or she is just going along with the "innocent friends" thing until the sex happens.

Sex with the mature female philanderer

Young men are of the opinion that a mature woman is somehow grateful for their attention. Wrong answer, they are grateful for the good or great sex. They can train you to give them the type of sex how they want it and when they want it.

Listen up young bucks, if she is married, she is not going to leave her hard working, great provider, vested in his pension plan husband for you. If he is not a hard-working good provider husband and she is constantly complaining about him, then he has something she wants or she would have left him a long time ago. Unless you can offer a mature, married, female philanderer more than she is getting from her spouse, you might as well smile and be happy with what you're getting. Your dick may swing her way, but it is never going to be enough motivation for her to leave her spouse. The bottom line is that she enjoys what the two of you have, just the way she is getting it, therefore she is not going to rock the boat, just so she must swim to shore. Granted she may have told you all the things your young ears want to hear but it was just that, talk.

Sex and the mature male philanderer

Young women have the same outlook on life with a mature male philanderer that young men do. He is going to leave his housekeeping, soccer mom, mother of his adult children, beloved Grandma, cooking, take his medication reminding wife and married to him for more years than you have been alive, for you just because you have a great body, and the sex is good or even great.

Well let me put your young mind at ease. He is Beelzebub's brother Sugar Daddy, and he is not going to leave his wife. You are a great lay, his frequent vacation from is everyday life, but like all great vacations, they end at some point, and so he returns home to his wife. He enjoys spending time with you because it makes him feel young again, so he has some affection for you.

So, you have one of two choices: 1 stop sleeping with married men or 2 take what you're getting and quit bitching. Money, sex, and some of his time is what you were asking for, you wanted to be his Satan sister Semi Pro now you are so don't complain because he will not give you more.

Part 10
A Word to Mister and Mistress

This is an example of how small a large city can be: I worked for a small company for three years and got to know one of my coworkers well. She told me about her husband and daughter daily for the years that we worked together. When I left the company, I became employed with another small company. One of the two women I was employed with at this new company started telling me about her married boyfriend and his daughter and his wife. From the description of him and his family I knew that it was the spouse of my former coworker. I had seen and talked to him when I was employed with his wife.

Like Satan's sister Gullible this mistress was under the impression that her mister needed her and that as some point he would leave his wife of almost 18 years for her. I on the other hand knew that this would never happen because mister had too much to lose. As of the publication of this guide mister was still with his wife.

I am telling you this story as an example of how easily you can be caught cheating and how some people that you are cheating with are so willing to talk about it to anyone.

"Six degrees of separation" is the idea/concept that there are only six things or people standing between you and a situation or a person that you are familiar with. My former coworker introduced me to her spouse. Her spouse introduced me to the headhunter that got me the new position. The headhunter in turn introduced me to the mistress of my former coworker. As you can see that situation only took three degrees.

My new co-worker was a prime example of Satan's sister Semi Pro. She only dated married men of means. I had worked with her for less than a month and had gotten all the information I could have ever needed if I had wanted to make for the would-be philanderer. Can you imagine the different levels of hell I could have taken him to if I had informed my former co-worker that I could introduce her to her spouse's mistress?

There is a line from an old R&B song by a man named Johnny Taylor that goes… "it's cheaper to keep her, it cost too much to leave her alone." No truer words have ever been spoken. One thing that all misters and mistress' need to understand is that husbands and wives more often than not don't leave their spouses to be with the person that they are philandering with. As I stated before there are exceptions to every rule and this one is no different.

Part 11
The Conclusion

Now that you have finished this guide, I know what
you're thinking…., "she's wrong, this is not just about
sex in my secondary relationship". "I really love my
mister or mistress". "I stay in my primary relationship
because of the kids, or she needs me". Or a whole
host of other nonsense justifications that you've given
yourself when you look in the mirror each morning.

But the truth is that you want your primary relationship,
if it were really that bad or unsatisfying you would have
been gone a long time ago. Your life is not going to
change if you don't change it. So, if you have purchased
this book for that reason then you need to know that
this book was written to inform you about life choices
and not to make life choices for you.

If you are going to develop a secondary relationship,
make sure that you are armed with all the required
knowledge to handle that life successfully.

Before you start any relationship review your primary
life carefully to make sure that you are making the

correct choice for yourself and not because you know of someone that has a secondary life.

After all, if someone else knows about it they're not successful.

I have told you all the things that you should not do when you're philandering, now I am going to tell you all the things you need to do.

1. Get an answering service. This is the telephone number that you will give your mister or mistress so that they may contact you.

2. I told you previously in this guide that it is a bad idea to give your mister or mistress access to your primary life.

3. Get a prepaid credit or debit card with paperless billing and statements. Be sure and link it to a telephone that your spouse does not have access to. Your local stores are full of them. This is the card that you will used to cover expenses with your mister or mistress.

4. If you have not joined the gym do so now. It will be a reason for you to be out of the house a few nights or days a week. If a gym is not your thing and your wife or husband knows it, then join another club that has meetings at night or at the weekends.

5. If your money is an issue and your spouse holds the purse strings, then get a small loan, or get an advance on your paycheck to cover for the answering service.

6. If your spouse has been wanting to join a club or a gym this is a very good time to encourage your spouse to do so. If your spouse spends two or three nights a week out of the house so much the better.

7. If you are going to be spending time at your mister or mistress' place, then it is a good idea to purchase the same hygiene products that you use at home. In addition, invest in unscented baby wipes for quick clean ups.

8. Purchase condoms, lots, and lots of condoms. Coming home with something that you did not leave with can get you killed not just divorced. For the stupid philanderer, do not leave them at home or in your car; sooner or later your spouse will find them there.

9. Purchase a prepaid cell phone so that you can call your mister or mistress. Do not take that phone to your personal residence. Leave it at work or hide it outside of your home but not in your car. Also never contact your spouse from this phone

When all else fails always refer to the five ultimate rules.

It is sad to say but, in this day and age, men and women have more opportunities to philander than ever before.

Because women make it too easy for men, and men are under the impression that no woman would ever cheat on them. These days women are more willing to share a man just for the sake of having a man or maybe just a part of a man a part of their time. Monogamy is still alive and well, but you need to see it when you have it and recognize it when you don't.

Of all the things that my dear departed grandmother taught me the most important of them all was this…, "let a word to the wise be sufficient". If you have been caught philandering in the past and you continue to philander in the same manner, you will be caught again.

Now that you have completed your reading, I would like for you to take the time to write down the pros and cons of your primary relationship. If you find that the pros are far more abundant than the cons, then maybe philandering is not where you should focus your energy.

In that same token if the cons are more abundant than the pros then take this book too heart and choose the best person to philander with among Satan Sisters or Beelzebub's Brothers.

You can philander successfully, but you must employ the rules and you must embrace the concept of two separate lives. Throughout the entire manual I have tried to teach you the process. It is why this book was written. Employ the rules, choose the right person, remember the general dues and don'ts, lie well and to the right person, manage your time and remember the philandering indicators. Keep these steps in mind and you will always be a successful philanderer if you choose to be. Now that we have come to the end of this manual, I would like you to take the time to take a look at your current situation and review your current relationship or relationships by writing down the pros and cons. When you are done, I believe that you will be able to make an informed decision about philandering.

P. S. Don't forget to destroy the Pros and Cons paper when you are done.

www.ingramcontent.com/pod-product-compliance
Lightning Source LLC
Chambersburg PA
CBHW060246030426
42335CB00014B/1608